For all of those who have suffered at the hands of

paedophiles, rapists and sexual predators.

It has been an honour to know and to work with so

many, the true warriors.

I hope that you find solace and help to get

through and to get on with the life that

you absolutely and emphatically deserve.

With Love from
'The Author'

Introduction;

Someone thought it was okay to take advantage of you, to hurt you and make you feel worthless......?

That doesn't make you weak or less of a person....the fact that you have survived such an attack makes you a warrior! Your body will react in ways to keep you safe from further harm.

You may not feel it right now, but with a bit of encouragement and the right assistance you may well start to think about your future in a way that you haven't felt able to for some time.

Every single day from now on, you can start to notice for yourself, subtle changes within you – maybe you will smile or laugh a bit more than you did. Small triumphs every day, okay?

Maybe you will start to feel ready to look up to the sky and to notice the blues and greens that are as ancient as life itself, rather than down to the ground where it's grey and dark.

Let the light shine in and in turn this will allow the light to begin to shine within you.

Triumph number 1 - YES

Write down five positive changes that you think you could make to start to help yourself...

1.

2.

3.

4.

5.

Five more triumphs for you.....YES

If you could write a song about your future, what would you call it and what would it be about?

Song Title: _____

Content:

Verse:

Psycho educational information – Jai Smith

Here's a story about a man called Jai Smith. He was walking through a Park in London, England, on his way to work one fine morning. It was April and the sun was shining. There were workers cutting the grass for the first time of the season. In the distance, children squealed and played happily in their red gingham spring dresses before school and people ambled about the park. Some were eating and drinking breakfast from paper plates and cups as they talked and laughed together, some sat on benches reading newspapers.

Suddenly, from nowhere, a German shepherd dog ran towards Jai and launched itself at his neck, ripping into his flesh, his body froze and he collapsed into a heap on the ground as the dog continued to rag him back and forth. Just as quickly as the dog had appeared, its' owner saw what was happening and called it, running off with it very quickly. People ran from every corner of the park to help him and an ambulance soon arrived to take him to hospital.

Within two weeks, he was feeling better, he knew he'd been very lucky to have survived the attack and was discharged from hospital with forty two stitches and two crutches. Jai had lots of practical support and recovered very well with the help of his friends and family, they never left him out or made him feel inadequate in any way.

Two years later, when Jai had been married for just over a year, his wife had asked him to take their tiny daughter Grace, out for a stroll in the buggy so that she could get some housework done. By now he lived in another town, far from London. As he walked up the street he noticed the familiar smell of fresh cut grass and he started to feel a bit odd but he couldn't understand why. He thought he might be coming down with a cold.

Not wanting to go home and disturb his wife so soon, he decided to keep walking and to go and have a look at the new Italian restaurant which had just opened at the top of the street. The new restaurant had two huge open panes of glass as shop frontage, allowing for full view of the dining area, as he looked through the window, his eyes focussed on the many red gingham tablecloths, his heart raced and he started to panic, he didn't know why at this point he just felt as if he couldn't breathe. His baby daughter was asleep and blissfully unaware as he sat down on some steps, desperately trying to calm down and to gather his thoughts. He was having a full blown panic attack, hardly able to breathe but he somehow managed to ring his wife, she came and took him home and he refused to leave the house for many weeks, which turned into months after that. Jai went to his doctor and was prescribed anti-depressants which consequently had their own side effects. His wife left the marital home to stay at her parents as she could not cope with his panic attacks and unreasonable behaviour.

Jai was unable to go to work and subsequently, after so much time of absence, he was relieved of his duties. In just over two years he had lost everything.

Terrorising Trauma Triggers

When a person has suffered a traumatic incident, such as rape and/or sexual violence, the brain takes in all of the information at the time and provides a technique called pattern matching, which, like a radar, reminds the person of all of the significant environmental information, just as the smell of the fresh cut grass and gingham table cloths affected Jai.

The pattern matching acts as a reminder of the possible dangers and that the last time Jai for example, smelled freshly cut grass or saw red gingham, his life was threatened. It is a perfectly normal response and is there to help us survive.

When a triggered moment occurs, your whole body may start to shake, heart may be pounding and you may feel dizzy and disorientated. Your mouth might be dry and you experience remembered terror like a distorted film running in your head.

Triggers can occur in many areas, sometimes it can be a telephone call or a colour even – that might be the same colour of the clothing worn by the perpetrator, it can be smells or tastes and even visual images of people who unfortunately look similar to the perpetrator/s who attacked you. The triggered memories can be so subtle but so overwhelming that you can feel unable to make sense of what is happening. This is normal, you are normal.

Paralysing Panic Attacks

You can suddenly hear your own heart beating and feel unable to breathe, so unfamiliar is it that you actually believe you are going to die, you are abreacting, in other words, the memory is so profound that it feels like you are back at the incident to the point where adrenaline has been released from your adrenal glands (situated above your kidneys).

Red blood cells flood to carry oxygen – blood is diverted to wherever it is needed. Your breathing has become rapid to provide you with more energy. Your lungs have dilated to give you more oxygen.

Sweating may have increased, and you are likely to feel sick, but you can't. You need the toilet badly, which is your body's way of making your body lighter for purposes of flight. Your muscles may have tightened and you are like a coiled spring. Your blood pressure may also be raised as your body reminds you of the terror that you experienced previously.

All of these body responses may be happening to you in a split second, even though it might feel and seems much longer. The silence in your head is often deafening as you endure these ruminations and memories, as your brain appears to be hijacked by what happened to you.

Horrible Hypervigilance

Jumping at every little sound, nerves on edge, constantly on high alert. The ripples of this can make not only you, but those around you, jumpy and over nervous. It is an enhanced state of awareness that primarily keeps you safe by reminding you of possible dangers that may be related to the incident. This is normal, you are normal.

Basically, your body is always on high alert and in preparation to fight or flight or freeze just as it did at the time of the traumatic incident. It can lead to an inability to function effectively in social situations, work or within academic environments.

Stressful Sleeplessness

There is nothing worse than going to bed, ready to get some sleep and then finding yourself just lying there, hour after hour.

The effects of lack of sleep can alter the mind as it tries to make sense of the world in a fog like state.

The long term effects of sleep deprivation are real, the body need a certain amount of rest to function at its optimum level. It is when the restoration of cells and chemical balances take place.

During the sleeping state, the brain rewires in accordance with the neurons that fire together and the processing of all waking state activity is processed into the appropriate part of the brain.

Without enough sleep, the brain and body systems won't function normally and sleep deprivation can be responsible for a lower quality of life.

There are many ways to readjust your sleep pattern to its normal regulatory system, however, if you have information such as images, thoughts, memories and emotions connected to the trauma, it may just be time to seek some post trauma therapy, which will help you to process the information that is keeping you wide awake.

REM – Rapid Eye Movement

Every night when we go to sleep, our brain is hardwired to take us through a rapid eye movement system, ensuring that we safely file away all the information received during the day.

When a person has suffered a traumatic event such as rape and/or sexual violation the consequential effects are often accompanied by disturbed sleep patterns.

During post trauma processing, such as EMDR, VKD or BSP the therapist will facilitate replication of the REM process whilst you are in the waking state.

This is how unprocessed information can be safely put away in the memory bank where it can be safely stored and with the earlier emotional impact lessened.

Healing Your Inner YOU

If you were sexually violated as a child, your mind and body may remember what happened to you and will seek to remind you whenever it is necessary to protect you from similar incidents or further harm.

This could play out in many ways such as an aversion to intimacy and/or sexual activity. Hatred towards certain people who may remind you of the abuser or who still have a relationship with them.

Embedded beliefs about your own developmental self-esteem and confidence, repeatedly having been told to keep secrets and often to have been preyed upon by sexual predators who will groom, coerce, manipulate, dominate, blackmail, tease, ridicule, finance, threaten or isolate in an underlying and underhand manner in which to abuse, assault and psychologically disempower tearing away at your basic human right to a childhood.

Sexual predators, who prey on children almost always put themselves in positions of authority, trust or are already family members, friends or relations.

Moving into adulthood, the fact that the physical/sexual touching and assaults have stopped can seem like the end, unfortunately, as you may be aware, this is not always the case; metaphorically, childhood sexual abuse can be likened to a deepening barbed splinter within the body, the more the 'victim' holds on to the 'secret' locked away inside – the deeper the splinter embeds and the sharper the barbs impale on their soul, leaving scars that, for many, seem impossible to heal.

On reflection, in later life, survivors look back at their abuse with the eyes of an adult and not the terror of a vulnerable child. It can often be too late to seek justice against the perpetrator/s but it is never too late to start to heal and with the right help, that metaphoric splinter can be gently and slowly removed.

It takes a huge amount of guts and courage for survivors of paedophiles and rapists to finally find a voice and speak out against those who have molested them and the recent disclosures about high profile abusers and child rapists have opened the floodgates, giving permission for others to do so in a safe and more accepted way, all of those affected by any form of sexual violation in childhood deserve the very best help they can get, even if for some, this is remaining safe within their silence.

EMPTY 'RAGE PAGE' EXERCISE......

Draw a picture of someone or something that has annoyed you today and rip it up into tiny pieces – dispose of as you wish and move on.....

Personal Reflective Journal Notes...

Colouring is an old favourite when you really don't feel like talking or actively engaging with others, giving time and space to be creative with colour and to reflect and imagine using new and positive thoughts. Finish the colouring, give your self-something small, to finish off. Triumph – YES

You may trod me in the very dirt
But still, like dust, I'll rise.
–Maya Angelou

Personal Reflective Journal Notes...

Three Thoughtful Mindfulness Techniques
Here and Now

Surprising Sixty Seconds

You'll need to find somewhere quiet where you won't be disturbed, where there are no disturbances, close your eyes and slowly count to ten.

As you breathe in, try and empty your mind and if you can do that without being disturbed or your mind wandering, then do it again for a slow count of twenty.

If you can do that – increase it to thirty, then when you can do that, increase it to forty and then fifty and then up to sixty.

Be at one with you, with who you really are on the inside.

Once you have mastered this breathing and mindfulness technique – you will be able to use it whenever or wherever you are.

K.O.G ~ Technique
Kinaesthetic, Olfactory, Gustatory

So, this is a technique that works with three of your senses, feelings, smells and taste.

Make yourself a hot drink – preferably a drink that is nurturing for you such as a healing tea or a cold refreshing drink, maybe organic.

You are worth the very best and your body deserves to be nurtured and strengthened.

Find a place where you feel safe, sit comfortably and breathe as per the previous technique.

When you are relaxed – take hold of the drink safely and with your eyes closed – get a physical sense of how you are sitting, take note of all of your body parts and make sure you are really comfortable.

Feel the temperature, whether hot or cold in your hands and the way it travels through the rest of your body.

When you are ready, take a sip of your chosen drink, notice the taste and how the liquid seeps down past your tongue and into your throat – concentrate on this here and now experience and notice your primeval senses, as they feel, taste and smell – keeping you in this moment.

Once you have mastered this you will slowly learn how to do this within your day to day existence and you will feel calmer, more aware and more in control of your body and how you feel.

Day to Day Mindfulness Techniques

Safety Assurance Technique

If you happen to be laying in your bath or doing any day to day normal function, start to assure yourself of how safe you are...for example

Okay, so I am washing my dishes...

The dishes in the sink of the house that I live in......

The house that I live in that has double glazing.....

The double glazing in the house that keeps me safe....

The safety that I feel now keeps me well and happy......

The happiness I feel is because I survived......

It is not happening now................

I am safe now...........

You can continue with this wherever you are and wherever your safety is nor compromised, but each time that you do it and speak out loud, you continually empower yourself further about how safe you are now...

Out with friends

In your car

At work

At college

In a supermarket

In a cinema

Nutrition and Exercise....

Trying to process trauma, expends a great strain on our equilibrium and general wellbeing – not to mention the cost to family and friends and relationships.

One of the best defences can only be to arm ourselves with good nutritious food. Cutting out sugary or chemically laden drinks and trying to get out for a brisk walk wherever possible.

We've made our own recipes for nutritious smoothies that will keep you motivated and energised for longer.

Empowering Energy Smoothie

Ingredients:

2 x Big Juicy Oranges (peeled)

2 x Bananas (peeled)

1 x Ruby red grapefruit (peeled)

2 x Carrots

Handful of Seedless Grapes

Large bio plain yoghurt – or Greek Yoghurt

Method:

Put all ingredients through the juicer, add yoghurt and fresh bottled spring water.

Place in flask or suitable container in the fridge to chill.

Take with you to drink throughout the day.

Research the best tasty ingredients to suit your own taste and/or find the help of an established nutritionist in your area.

EMPTY 'RAGE PAGE' EXERCISE......

Draw a picture of someone or something that has annoyed you today and rip it up into tiny pieces – dispose of as you wish and move on.....

I am perfectly entitled to be ME ~ Empowerment after Abuse and Violence

Tick or sign at the end of each line......

1. I have a right to recover from abuse, to be free to live my life, my way.................................

2. I have a right to spend time with my family and friends...

3. I have a right to decide what will help me or what won't...

4. I have a right to my personal space...

5. I have a right to recover at my own pace...

6. I have a right to wear what I choose...

7. I have a right to go where I choose...

8. I have a right to my own feelings and thoughts about what happened.............................

9. I have a right to make my own decisions...

10. I have a right to be me..

Personal Reflective Journal Notes...

You are not responsible
for other people's behaviour......

DOODLING-PAGE

Finish these sentences.........

If I could have one month off and still get paid I would go to.........

_____

_____

_____

_____

_____

_____

_____

If I won eighteen million on the lottery, I would..............

_____

_____

_____

_____

_____

_____

If I could change anything about my future now, I would...............

_____

_____

_____

_____

_____

_____

_____

Trauma Tapestry: A Seven-Step Process

All you need to do here......is develop your own picture – only you have the images of what happened to you – it doesn't matter whether you can draw or not, this is about putting all the pieces together and making sense of exactly what happened to you....

1.   *So, you just start to draw whatever the strongest images are for you or write whatever you feel needs writing.*

2.   *Over time and when you are ready, start to join the pictures together with tape in exactly the order that YOU think they should be.*

3.   *When you have completed the paper tapestry you need to SAFELY burn it (a baking tray or a wok, works wonders) but you need to keep the ash.*

4.   *Then you just need to decide what you would like to do with the ash.*

Some ideas might be.....

5.   *Put ashes into a pot or into the earth and grow a plant so that something beautiful grows from something not so beautiful.*

6.   *Put ashes into a piece of muslin, tie to an air balloon and let it go, watch until it disappears out of sight.*

7.   *Take the ashes in a box or an envelope to a significant place or the where the assault happened and leave, bury or scatter them there.*

8.   *Put ashes in the toilet, skip, rubbish dump anywhere that is significant.*

9.   *Release ashes into a river or stream (making sure there is no plastic contained within them).*

One enormous and beautiful triumph for you once this has been done
YES......

Finished....YES! And.........Another Triumph – YES!!

'Success is never final. Failure is never fatal.
It is courage that counts'
Winston Churchill

Forgive yourself.......

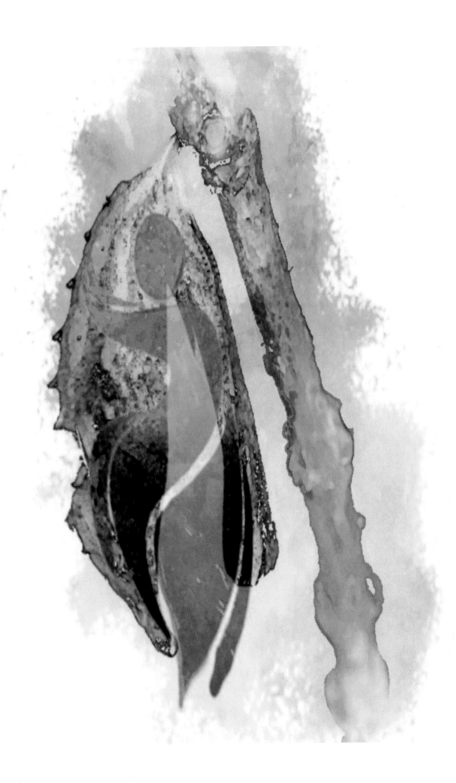

Now is not forever – you will survive this....

Short Visualisation Exercise – Empowered Self

You may need a friend or someone you trust to help you with this and read out the script below.......all you need to do is listen, follow and create your empowered self.

Think of a recent incident where you were not able to handle the situation in a way that you would have liked. This is a short intervention that will help you with future reactions. You can keep your eyes open or closed throughout. Okay so just place on the inner screen of your mind – an image of YOUR Empowered Self.

This is not a picture of you at your most assertive. It is though a picture of a self that you have not yet even become. This self has developed to such a degree, that you have all the skills, knowledge and choices in life to feel safe, nurtured and be in full control of yourself in life. Okay so once you have a picture there on your inner screen of your **EMPOWERED SELF**

- That's excellent – okay now you can spend a little time building up a clearer picture of your ES.

- Tell me what you notice about your ES that is possibly different from the way you are today – is he/she older – sitting – standing? Where they are and what are they doing?

- So let yourself elaborate a bit:

- What is your hair like?

- What is your face like?

- What clothes do you wear – colour – texture – style

- Become aware of your Empowered Self's facial expressions

- How does your ES feel?

- When you look at your ES what gives this away to you – how do you know?

- How does your ES feel towards others?

- When you look at your ES what gives this away to you – how do you know?

- How do others feel towards your ES?

- When you look at your ES, what gives this away to you – how do you know?

- How does your ES feel towards and about him/herself?

- When you look at your ES what gives this away to you – how do you know?

- ON a day-to-day basis what does you ES say to self?

- When you look at your ES what gives this away to you – how do you know?

- What does your ES fundamentally believe about them self?

- When you look at your ES what gives this away to you – how do you know?

Ask your friend to or check your own responses – check out if anything has been missed:

So, when all is confirmed, just imagine going to the screen and simply stepping inside of your ES – when you are there you will simply be inside your ES's body, looking out of the same eyes – just feel what it feels like to be in there.

Confirm when you are there.

Once you have confirmed to yourself or to a friend – when you think about that incident the one where you were not able to handle it as you would have liked: just re –run it in the inner screen of your mind and then get a sense of how your ES handles the situation and what it feels like.

Remember that you are simply just along for the ride – an observer if you like.

So when you are ready, simply re run the scene from its beginning through to its natural conclusion until it's complete.

Make sure you have stepped out of your ES and just be YOU again bringing your awareness back to your current space.

Were you able to do that? DISCUSS with a friend or counsellor or family member......

And another massive Triumph YES

Remember that it is your choice to heal, once you take responsibility to seek healing for yourself, you accept that you are worth the time and effort involved, to make positive changes in your life.

You are not going mad – you are reacting normally to an abnormal situation...

It's always your choice to work towards post traumatic growth.....

When you take responsibility to seek healing for yourself, you accept that you are worth the time and effort involved to make positive changes in your life.

This is a brave first step, the first of many, on the road to recovery.

You may begin to doubt your own memory or deny the reality and severity of the incident/s. This did happen to you and YOU DID NOT cause it to happen.

"I can be changed by what happens to me, but I refuse to be reduced by it"

Maya Angelou

Crossword - Time to use your little grey cells and work this out....

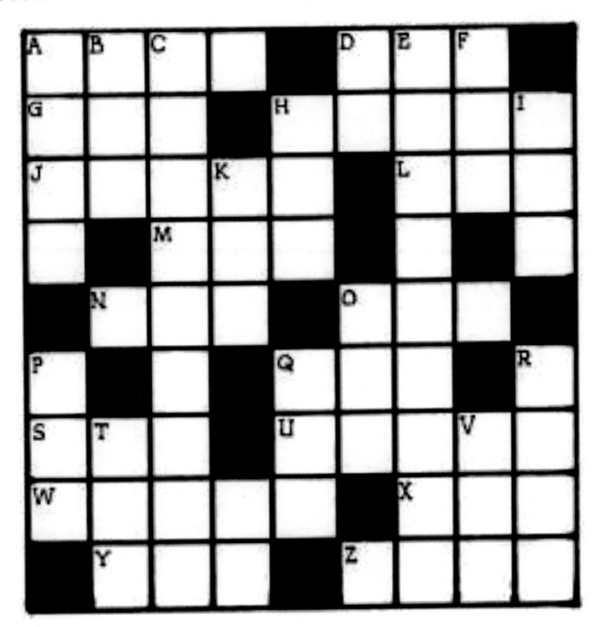

Across Clues.

A. A place to relax in water
D. Suffix to form a noun
G. Remnants of fire
H. Dramatic work set to music
J. Homeless person in New York
L. Be able to
M. Colour of confidence or anger

N. *Purring friend/foe*
O. *Adams' woman*
Q. *Before – definition*
S. *Beautiful large fish*
U. *Inaccuracy*
W. *Placed within another*
X. *Tree prone to disease*
Y. *Acronym for arrival time*
Z. *Lyrical poems*

Down Clues.

A. *Lowest part of something*
B. *To question*
C. *Talking professional*
E. *To be well again*
F. *Long and distant period in history*
H. *Not young*
I. *A number of things*
K. *Allow to happen*
O. *To make a mistake*
P. *Sport in the snow*
R. *Could be loving and/or strong*
T. *Singular*
V. *Spanish exclamation of approval*

Completed Crossword?

Beautiful triumph here...........YES!!

What people might be saying – never worry about the opinions or judgements of others, what they think and say is part of their own reality; it's not yours, it's totally irrelevant.

Others input is simply not important, they were not present during the sexual attack, they have not walked your path and they are not your judge.

Professional Help

If you decide to seek professional help, there are certain researched and effective treatments that can help you to work through the trauma that you have endured.....

Here we mention a few of the best......

Eye Movement Desensitisation Reprocessing (EMDR)

Eye Movement Desensitisation Reprocessing (more commonly known as EMDR), is a form of psychotherapy developed in the 1980s by American psychologist Francine Shapiro.

During a stroll in the park, Shapiro made a chance observation that certain eye movements appeared to reduce the negative emotion associated with her own traumatic memories.

When she experimented, she found that others also exhibited a similar response to eye movements, and so she set about conducting controlled studies before developing a multiphase approach to trauma reduction.

Researched and evidenced intervention for multiple traumas to suit individuals who were sexually abused over a period of time in their childhood, the treatment itself can help a survivor of sexual abuse to release the unprocessed information, traumatic and distressing images, body memories and intense feelings.

It can lessen the impact and allow the client to be free of the 'trauma fog' that may have taken up so much of their thinking time.

If you have been raped or sexually violated, the memory of your traumatic experience may come hurtling back into your mind like a racing tide, pushing you to re-experience the original incident with the same intensity of feeling - like it is taking place in the present moment.

While it isn't possible to erase these memories completely, the process of Eye Movement Desensitisation Reprocessing (EMDR) can lessen the impact and rearrange the storage of such memories, allowing you to recall them with less emotion or distress.

There are eight phases to this trauma treatment as follows:

1. History taking often with a time line, symptoms and units of distress, consideration of whether or not EMDR is the best course of action for you and whether or not you are sufficiently resourced to receive it.

2. Preparation for treatment may include, demonstration with tapping techniques, breathing techniques, answering any questions and generally preparing you for your first session.

3-6. From phase three to approximately six, from your initial time line of traumatic incidents, you can start to choose where you would like to start, you will be asked to answer some questions that relate to the incident, which will require positive and negative answers and different sensory responses will be questioned, you will be completely free to choose the exact incident that you feel comfortable with. The EMDR sessions can be provided with hand movements, or bi lateral stimulation, using a set of tappers or light sensory units. These are divided into sets and after each set, you will be asked for feedback. The whole intervention is based on lowering your SUDS (subjective units of distress) and lessening the impact for you.

7. The therapist will manage the time in the session so that you finish with a safe place which allows you to feel calmer before leaving.

8. The eight phase, gives you an opportunity to re-evaluate and to make sure all is going well for you and where you need to work to continue with lessening the impact or if you are able to work on a different issue.

Following EMDR, processing will continue as your brain assimilates and integrates all the information.

This is a positive sign that material is being processed.

Below are examples of what other clients have described between sessions.
If this is a road you decide to travel, you may want to make a note of any changes that you experience.

- *You may feel exhausted or more tired than usual.*
- *You may be full of vibrant energy.*
- *Some people experience physical reactions such as a headache or a cold like symptoms.*
- *Some people report a mushy type feeling in their head.*
- *You may feel lighter and have a spring in your step.*
- *You may get a sense that something has changed, but you are not sure what.*
- *You may experience a temporary loss of concentration while your mind resettles.*
- *You may experience a few hollow memories of the session but this will be temporary.*
- *You may be more emotional or less – it is all part of the processing.*
- *New forgotten memories may surface and unsettle you for a time.*
- *Processing will continues after the session and you may experience more details as it does.*
- *You may experience more intense dreams that you are able to remember*

Although this list is by no means complete, the reactions are all a perfectly normal part of EMDR.

Brain spotting (BSP)

A powerful, focused treatment method that works by identifying, processing and releasing core neurophysiological sources of emotional/body pain, trauma, dissociation and a variety of other challenging symptoms.

Brainspotting is a simultaneous form of diagnosis and treatment, enhanced with bio lateral sound, which is deep, direct, and powerful yet focused and containing.

This is a relatively new intervention which works on the basis of releasing the **body** from the traumatic memories it holds via the neurobiological pathway.

It is an excellent and useful tool for working with adult survivors of sexual assault, because it is non-invasive and the client doesn't necessarily need to speak.

This technique allows the body to tell the story and in doing so can release many years of pent up stagnant and toxic agony.

Brainspotting functions as a neurobiological tool to support the clinical healing relationship.

There is no replacement for a mature, nurturing therapeutic presence and the ability to engage another suffering human in a safe and trusting relationship where they feel heard, accepted, and understood.

Brainspotting gives us a tool, within this clinical relationship, to a neurobiological location, focus, process, and to release experiences and symptoms that are typically out of reach of the conscious mind and its cognitive and language capacity.

Brainspotting works with the deep brain and the **body** through its direct access to the autonomic and limbic systems within the body's central nervous system. Brainspotting is accordingly a physiological tool/treatment, which has profound psychological, emotional, and physical consequences.

It is theorized that Brainspotting taps into and harnesses the body's innate self-scanning capacity to process and release focused areas (systems), which are in a maladaptive homeostasis (frozen primitive survival modes). This may also explain the ability of Brainspotting to often reduce and eliminate body pain and tension associated with physical conditions.

Visual Kinesthetic Dissociation Technique (VKD)

This is a specific intervention for traumatic incident, such as rape and sexual violence, the rewind technique, also known as the fast phobia cure, evolved from the technique developed by Richard Bandler one of the co-founders of Neuro Linguistic Programming (NLP). He called it the VK dissociation technique (the V stands for visual and the K for kinesthetic — feelings).

The version recommended by the European Therapy Studies Institute has been refined and streamlined, as a result of its own research into why and how best it works. It is highly useful for individuals who, after exposure to traumatic events, have developed PTSD or lesser forms of the condition.

Simply described, the technique works by allowing the traumatised individual, whilst in a safe relaxed state, to reprocess the traumatic memory so that it becomes stored as an 'ordinary', albeit unpleasant, and non- threatening memory rather than one that continually activates a terror response.

This is achieved by enabling the memory to be shifted in the brain from the amygdala to the neocortex.

The amygdala's role is to alert us to danger and stimulate the body's 'fight or flight' reaction.

Normally, all initial sensations associated with a threatening experience are passed to the amygdala and formed into a sensory memory, which in turn is passed on to the hippocampus and from there to the neocortex where it is translated into a verbal or narrative memory and stored.

When an event appears life- threatening, however, there can be sudden information overload and the sensory memories stay trapped in the amygdala instead of being passed on to, and made sense of by, the neocortex.

While trapped in the amygdala, the trauma memory has no identifiable meaning.

It cannot be described, only re-experienced in some sensory form, such as panic attacks or flashbacks.

The rewind technique allows that sensory memory to be converted into narrative, and be put into perspective. It is our sense that trauma is often seen within the mental health profession as a long-term problem, and is perhaps more often misdiagnosed than diagnosed.

Rewind, however, puts a trauma into perspective very neatly.

The treatment takes only a short time; perhaps close to the length of time the incident took to occur — a terrible experience but a tiny part of an entire life.

By relocating the traumatic memory from one part of the brain to another — the place where it was meant to end up in the first place, it re-balances the experience within a person's life.

Most of the people we work with just want to put their experience into proper perspective, not suffer symptoms any more, and get on with their lives.

Rewind is not only powerfully effective in that respect, but side effect free.

Relaxation and/or Mindfulness

Both of these are popular for those working within the field of trauma and usually at the first couple of sessions to teach the client how to ground themselves and be relaxed.

Only by remaining calm can you even begin to quiet the chaos of a damaged psyche.

These could be used alongside other treatments, i.e. the Rewind technique works twice as well if combined with a deep relaxation process, as does Critical Incident Debriefing with individuals.

Mindful relaxation can have a powerful impact on our ability to work towards a longer life, to really feel and see what is before us, awareness of such really is the cornerstone of healing and recovery.

Because the brain is in a hi-jacked state in the aftermath of a traumatic sexual assault, those affected may find it more difficult to break down the fog and to accomplish relaxation.

Sensorimotor Psychotherapy

Those affected by rape and sexual violence often carry the trauma within the very cells and muscular system of their body and it can feel difficult to feel safe again.

Engaging with therapies that offer a combined processing model of release for both the mind and body is crucial for moving forward.

Sensorimotor Psychotherapy is a therapy developed by Dr Pat Ogden that works somatically (physiological memory) with both the mind and body, so that the traumatic memory can be processed effectively, allowing for lessened impact, thus leaving no residue of the traumatic memory.

The body, for a host of reasons, has been left out of the "talking cure."

Psychotherapists who have been trained in models of psychodynamic, psychoanalytic, or cognitive therapeutic approaches are skilled at listening to the language and effect of the client.

They track the clients' associations, fantasies, and signs of psychic conflict, distress, and defences.

Yet while the majority of therapists are trained to notice the appearance and even the movements of the client's body, thoughtful engagement with the client's embodied experience has remained peripheral to traditional therapeutic interventions.

Guided Visualisation

This is very powerful tool to assist clients especially when dealing with childhood trauma, such as sexual assault. It allows the client to go back, to revisit, and to make changes in situations that they were not able to do anything about as children.

It's useful to have some music in the background, and if possible, soft blankets available on offer, as many people feel quite exposed when they have their eyes closed.

There are CD's and productions developed to assist those affected by rape and sexual violation to find some peace and release from what they have endured. Intended as a stepping-stone along the passage of healing and recovery.

Like a tidal wave, the effects of childhood sexual abuse can saturate an adult throughout their life, Guided Visualisation allows the choice of time and space in the safety of one's own environment where disturbance can be minimal and relaxation can be attained in order to feel the letting go of many painful memories.

CID - Critical Incident Debriefing or Psychological Debriefing

This a psychological intervention implemented after a major incident. The aim of Critical Incident Debriefing (CID) is to prevent or limit the onset of Post-Traumatic Stress Disorder (PTSD) ideally; this intervention will take place within two to three days after the incident but can be still be beneficial many years after the event.

Debriefing was originally developed for the benefit of emergency services and military personnel but are now available to benefit the general population where they are exposed to a traumatic incident.

The most common model employed by debriefers is the Mitchell and Dyregrove model.

This consists of a seven-stage process which people are guided through by the debriefer/s. It can be used on groups of people or with individuals.

Cognitive Behavioural Therapy

Cognitive Behavioural Therapy (CBT) is a psychological treatment for mental health conditions. Treatment usually takes between eight and twenty sessions. It is a combination of cognitive therapy, which can modify or eliminate unwanted thoughts and beliefs, and behavioural therapy, which may help to change behaviour in response to those thoughts.

Cognitive techniques (such as challenging negative thoughts) and behavioural techniques (such as exposure therapy that gradually desensitises phobia and relaxation techniques) are used to relieve symptoms of anxiety and depression by changing thoughts, beliefs and behaviour.

CBT is based on the assumption that most unwanted thinking patterns and emotional and behavioural reactions are learned over a long period of time. The aim is to identify the thinking that is causing unwanted feelings and behaviours and to learn to replace this thinking with more positive thoughts. The therapist does not focus on the events from the past (such as childhood) but focuses on current difficulties at the present time. The therapist will be able to teach new skills and new ways of reacting.

EFT – Emotional Freedom Technique

This is an energy healing technique which is based upon the balance within our mind and body. All living creatures need certain elements to sustain life, without these elements such as food, water, love, company, life will cease and on the way the body will become distressed, physically distorted with a myriad of illness and disease and completely unable to function at any kind of normal level.

EFT is effective in restoring balance which consequentially allows the body and brain to seek further assistance in order to function fully again.

This intervention is known to release symptoms with a pattern of tapping with the fingertips on certain areas of the body which do actually correspond to acupuncture points on the energy meridians.

Where there is an imbalance, there is a corresponding blockage in the flow of energy through the meridian system.

Tapping points are as follows:

- Eyebrow
- Side of eye
- Under eye
- Under nose
- Chin
- Collar bone
- Karate chop point on side of hand
- Under arm

The tapping helps to release the blockages that were originally established at the source of the traumatic event.

Tapping allows the blockage to be released and balance can be restored. This works by processing the original unprocessed information stored in the body.

Massage Therapy & Yoga

One of the ways to assist with releasing the psoas muscle is with massage therapy, it can offer a deep sense of peace and relaxation for those who feel strong enough to just let it happen. Those burdened with the traumatic effects of continued sexual violation and assault on their bodies can find it difficult to 'let go' as their parasympathetic nervous system continually raises the danger alarm at touch of any kind.

If the client and massage therapist can build a rapport and enough trust to let the treatment commence then this can be a unique type of intervention.

A primary connector between the torso and the leg, the psoas is also an important muscle which affects posture, helps stabilize the spine, and, if it's out of balance, can be a significant contributor to low back and pelvic pain.

The way that the psoas is used in yoga practice can help keep it healthy, strong, and flexible.

Trauma informed yoga is useful in that the teacher will be appropriately trained and professionally informed and aware about triggers, those who dissociate and become easily emotionally overwhelmed and fully competent to assist with those who may experience flashbacks. The teacher will always be able to make time for you and will be mindful of the safety aspects surrounding the aftermath of those affected by trauma.

Bowen Technician & Energy Healing Therapies

As Bowen practitioners, the accuracy and the forgiveness applying the Bowen moves anatomically allow both the practitioner and client to be at optimum calmness, providing an environment to explore exactly how their body is responding to challenges in their life, environment, work and help to understand their stress patterns which can be reflected in their physiological presentations.

Once we move to understanding and witnessing this in the human form the Bowen work can be more directed and results as stated by the clients themselves, observed.

In order for our clients to start the healing and to process the trauma that they have endured, they need to be resourced (stable) enough to undergo the intensive and often emotionally turbulent interventions, working towards post traumatic growth.

Krav Maga

For those who feel they need to learn a self defence strategy that is effective and not combative, there is value in researching a class, enrolling and learning the Krav Maga system which is based on principles and concepts.

The system teaches how to defeat unarmed attackers and to deal with guns and knives. It also teaches how to debilitate attackers no matter how big they are which is an excellent skill to have and gives a target of a violent sexual predator, an extra chance to get away.

It was developed by the son of a Police Chief Inspector in Bratislava. Most importantly the system can be learned quickly and applied under extreme stress. The system is based on simple and reflexive moves that work when needed. As a constantly evolving system the effectiveness of techniques is constantly tested, evaluated and developed.

Goju-ryu

This is a traditional Okinawan style of karate with an extensive history. The term Goju-ryu actually means "hard-soft style," which refers to the closed hand techniques (hard) and open hand techniques and circular movements (soft) that comprise this martial art.

The basic goal of Goju-ryu karate is self-defence. It is primarily a stand up form that teaches practitioners how to block strikes by using angles, and then subdue them with hand and leg strikes. The art also teaches some takedowns, which tend to set up finishing strikes.

Rape Crisis Centres

If there is anywhere where you will most definitely be believed, supported and given plenty of support, it is at your nearest rape centre, male centres are gradually popping up all over the world and all can be located via a simple internet search. In the United Kingdom there are forty five organisations that are members of Rape Crisis, providing services in 56 locations across England and Wales.

Internationally, many services can be found by following this link http://www.ibiblio.org/rcip/internl.html

There are thousands more support services also available and these can be found by a quick internet search or via the DABS network (Directory of Abuse Book Services). http://dabs.uk.com/

Also, there are many counsellors and psychotherapists who are trained to work with sexually related assaults and you can find them here http://www.counselling-directory.org.uk/ you just need to put your postcode in the search bar and it will bring up the counsellors and therapists who are nearest to you, once you have completed this part, you can scroll through each members qualifications to see the most suitable person for your issues.

It was as late as 1973 that the first rape crisis centre actually opened and they have been progressively opening up across the country, initially, just for women and girls, more and more services are opening up to recognise the sexual violations of male survivors.

SARC - Sexual Assault Referral Centre

These provide services to victims/survivors of rape or sexual assault regardless of whether the survivor/victim chooses to reports the offence to the police or not. Some SARCs are not funded to provide support if there is no criminal investigation taking place but a referral to a Rape Crisis or similar service is often put in place and some may also offer their own or signposting to appropriate counselling and trauma focused therapy services. These excellent centres are designed to be comfortable and multi-functional, providing private space for interviews and examinations, all staff are trained to help you make informed decisions about what you want to do next.

ISVAs

Rape Centres and many specialist support agencies offer an **Independent Sexual Violence Adviser** (ISVA) service to those affected by rape and sexual assault. The Independent Sexual Violence Adviser role was commissioned by Baroness Stern through the Home Office Violent Crime Unit in 2005 and has proved to be an essential part of assistance.

ISVA's undergo specialist training and are equipped to address your needs and to provide support. An ISVA is trained to look after your needs, and to make sure that you are given the appropriate attention and consideration, helping you to go through the criminal process and to gain an understanding of how it works. They are able to help you and answer any questions that you may have. An ISVA is there to provide you with information only so that you can make the right decision for you. By contacting them, you are *not* expected to report any offence to the police.

Report a rape or sexual assault

If you're the victim of rape or sexual assault, the police and other organisations are there to help.

Call 999 to report a rape or attempted sexual assault, as soon as possible after the crime.

If the offence has recently happened:

- keep the clothes you were wearing and don't wash them - the police may need them as evidence for the investigation

- try not to shower as there may be evidence which the police can use

If you're under 17, the Child Protection Unit of your local police station will deal with your case.

What happens next?

The police (if you have reported it to them) or SARC staff will:

- arrange for you to have a medical examination - and treatment for any injuries you have
- give you support and advice
- explain what happens next
- provide details of other services who may assist you

Many police forces in the UK and Ireland have specialist teams who are trained to deal with rape and sexual assault.

When looking for a professional – take note of the following do's and don'ts – they might help you to find the right person for you.

1. Do expect to be listened to effectively, so that if the professional had to recall your story they would be able to without leaving anything out.

2. Do expect your experience to be acknowledged, understood and your recollection of events believed.

3. Make sure that you know how the professional will work with you so that you know what to expect and which aims you are working towards.

4. Don't be put under pressure to work faster than you are prepared to ~ you need to work at a pace to suit you.

5. The professional may offer you a terms and conditions or contractual agreement that will lay out the ethical boundaries under which they work, be sure to read them thoroughly so that you know what is expected of you in terms of cancellation policy etc.

6. The professional should under no circumstances, talk about their own issues, experience or life – the sessions are about YOU.

7. Ensure that the professional you are working with is fully qualified, it is okay to ask or search for information about them on the internet.

8. Expect to NOT be judged or told what to do next, if the professional that you have chosen does not seem able to assist you then they may know someone who can. Not every therapist is trained to work with rape and sexual violence.

That's another huge triumph for YOU – in just deciding whether or not you need professional help just to get through some of the unfinished stuff.

Remember.........that time really does accelerate healing, as you transcend into acceptance of what cannot be changed and work towards newness.

Quick Word Search

A	M	H	A	P	P	Y	V	X	O	Y	G
Y	O	E	M	P	O	W	E	R	E	D	Y
L	O	V	E	Z	S	C	R	P	Z	I	T
O	D	A	B	P	I	T	Y	O	V	S	G
Z	P	L	I	P	T	I	C	K	E	T	S
E	T	I	Z	A	I	M	S	E	T	R	Y
N	R	A	L	I	V	E	N	R	E	E	D
G	E	N	T	N	I	D	G	B	R	S	I
E	A	T	W	T	T	X	N	I	A	S	Z
N	T	P	I	E	Y	E	A	R	N	I	Z
R	E	O	F	N	X	V	T	D	U	N	Y
E	D	T	E	G	C	E	L	L	S	G	K

HAPPY, AIMS, LOVE, PITY, LIP, TICKETS, TRY, ALIVE, REED, GENT, EAT, EYE, YEARN, CELLS, MOOD, POSITIVITY, VERY, VALIANT, TREATED, PAINTING, LOZENGE, POKER, EMPOWERED, VETERAN, KERB, DISTRESSING, TIMED, DIZZY, BIRD, WIFE, GNAT, GENRE, EVE

And more colouring and relaxing – just for you, to indulge yourself in complete self-focus and creation of colours while you do so......

"If you hear a voice within you say you cannot paint, then by all means paint and that voice will be silenced."
Vincent van Gogh

Personal Reflective Journal Notes...

A Glimpse of Your Empowered Self

When a person survives a physical attack, in whatever way that is, they can often forget who they were before it happened. And what is important is that if you let it, allow it to shine through a NEW and exciting, stronger YOU can emerge from the aftershock.

- Close your eyes and if appropriate you can play some relaxing music in the background, you need feel safe and secure with this exercise.

- Use some breathing techniques such as breathing through your nose into your diaphragm for the count of seven and to breathe out for the count of eleven. Maybe do this three or four times.

- When you are relaxed you can ask a friend to ask you the following leading visualisation.

- Think of your life now but without the violence, physical and emotional pain and chaos.

- Who are you in the here and now today?

- What does that feel like?

- What does that look like?

- Imagine a version of yourself as YOUR new and empowered self.

- Imagine that vision as a clean living well healed version of YOUR true self.

- Look at YOUR new empowered self and see into YOUR heart, asking YOUR dreams and future plans.

- Take a while to allow the image to fill with colour, for rest and relaxation to work its way throughout YOUR entire body.

- So now just imagine walking down a road as YOUR empowered self, towards a fork in the road, if YOU go down the left fork YOU will undoubtedly return to a place where you are not yet ready to start to heal. What does that look like?

- So now what would it look like if YOU were to go down the right road, the right fork in the road, where YOU are in control of YOUR own decisions, and empowered to the highest that a person can possibly be.

- What does that freedom look like? This free new and empowered self is YOUR next chapter and future!

- So now just continue to make the image of YOUR empowered self as vibrant and strong as YOU possibly can and to hang in to it. YOU can add music to it or imagine carrying out an activity with a new sense of freedom and confidence in the way that YOU can envisage.

- So continue with what YOU have imagined and try to put it into practice and actually start to feel what it might be like to be YOUR empowered self and what life would be like as that free and empowered person.

Another complete triumph for you......

Personal Reflective Journal Notes...

Ten Beautiful Tips for Getting through Trauma.

1. Learn to breathe slowly through your nose and into your abdomen for the count of seven, and then slowly and determinedly, breathe out of your mouth for the count of eleven.

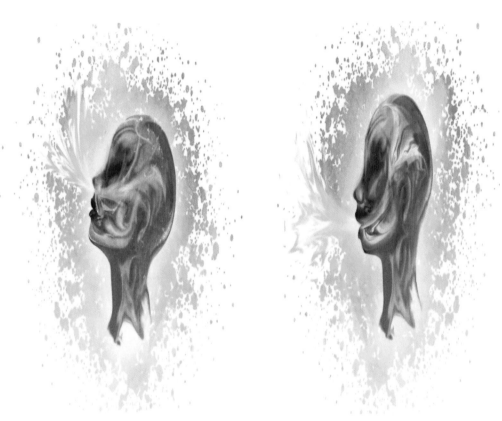

Count of 7 in through the nose   Count of 11 out through the mouth

7/11 Breathing

Breath in through the nose for the count of 7 *(blow up your stomach)*
Breath out through the mouth for the count of 11 *(empty stomach)*
It is the out breath that induces the calm.

Personal Reflective Journal Notes...

2. Become aware of how your body is responding to what happened to you. Your body holds onto the traumatic incident/s, as well as your brain.

If you decide that professional help is what you need, it is important that you find a therapist who is trained and competent to facilitate all areas of processing the traumatic information that is stored in your body.

Personal Reflective Journal Notes...

3. Find and tell someone who you trust, who you know will believe you, tell them what has happened to you, allow them to help and support you throughout your recovery process and beyond.

Remember that you are reacting normally to a completely abnormal situation.

Personal Reflective Journal Notes...

4. Your brain has been temporarily taken over by the traumatic event/s that you have endured, the traumatic information will need to be processed intensively for the impact to lessen. This will allow your brain to clear so that you can think clearly and begin to live again.

A trained therapist (and there are many, all over the world) will be able to work with you to facilitate the process safely and effectively.

Personal Reflective Journal Notes...

5. Learn to relax again, wherever possible, try to find some extra time to invest in yourself, go back to some of the activities that you used to enjoy or start new ones. If you can't already, learning to swim with a personal swim coach can allow for confidence and balance – both in body and mind.

This is about YOU and the strength of the person you are becoming.

Personal Reflective Journal Notes...

6. Unfamiliar feelings can be healthy or toxic which may be addressed with a trained professional or even by reading many of the excellent book written on the subject.

Personal Reflective Journal Notes...

7. The traumatic incidents must not define who you are.

YOU are a unique, amazing and beautiful individual who has every right to be happy and to find a renewed sense of self in normal day to day functioning.

Personal Reflective Journal Notes...

8. Release is beautiful, find a way to let it go, to restore your life for you, to the joy that it can be, seek, keep searching and you will find the right way to heal for you.

Above all, don't let anyone rush you, take your time, this is your journey, no one else's. All recovery needs to be at a pace that suits your needs.

Personal Reflective Journal Notes...

THE NOW YOU

Ideas to identity who you are **Now**....using taste, smell, feeling, thought and visual - all of your five senses **to create and establish the** NOW YOU.

1. Buy a brand new fragrant shower gel or soap that you've never used before such as strawberry or zesty lemon and associate this new scent with the NOW YOU.

2. Decide on a new colour scheme for your favourite room in your home.

3. Try a new food, associate the new taste with the NOW YOU.

4. Purchase the softest, warmest, cuddliest blanket for colder evenings in front of the television or with family and friends.

5. Eat and sleep well, nurture yourself, with good wholesome food. Try and get yourself back into a regular sleep pattern. Sleep is medicine for every cell in your body.

Sometimes it's good to research, find and purchase a new picture or wall canvas that makes you feel happy, for a favourite place in your home. Be kind to yourself, indulge yourself, in the NOW YOU.

Believe in YOU and the power that YOU hold, to recover and to get stronger every day.

We each create our own prisons, of which,
we each hold the key to be released.
Sue J. Daniels

Personal Reflective Journal Notes...

Personal Healing & Recovery Plan

(Name_____)

Foreword

YOUR thoughts of the last ten years - bullet pointed list of significant events.

Aims

One to five years ahead of what you want and need to achieve to make your life better for you.

1.

2.

3.

4.

5.

Personal Goals

Example

Personal Goal
e.g. **To cope better with what happened**

Lead Responsibility	Me
Others with Role to play	Therapist, Support Worker, Rape Crisis

	Work to be undertaken	Timescale	Status
1a	To research and find suitable therapist or support that will enable me commit to my own healing & recovery.	1 - 10 months	ONG
1b			
1c			

Status - Key	
A	Achieved
NA	Not Achieved
PA	Partly Achieved
ONG	Ongoing

You can add as many pages of personal goals as required

Life Goals

Example

Life Goal
To set up my own online business making cloth handbags.

Lead Responsibility	*Me*
Others with Role to play	*Bank*

	Work to be undertaken	Timescale	Status
2a	*To research the market*	*12 months*	*NA*
2b	*To speak to my bank and discuss options*	*6 months*	*NA*
2c			

Status - Key	
A	*Achieved*
NA	*Not Achieved*
PA	*Partly Achieved*
ONG	*Ongoing*

You can add as many pages of life goals as required

Full Plan

Full plan for the next ten years is...............realistic dreams that you can make become actual facts.

Stakeholders of my future plans & goals:

Family, spouse, children, who and what I invest in...

Most Important Priorities for me....

1.

2.

3.

4.

5.

6.

7.

8.

9.

10.

Give yourself time to heal.....to take time for yourself...

Rape is a violation of another person's rights, of their body and of their ability to make a choice.

Rape is about exerting power and control over another, using threats of physical violence, verbal threats and physical force...

Childhood rape and sexual assault....

Whether an individual or a group of abusers perpetrated the assaults, whether historical or recent.

The 'SECRET' may have been covered up because of fear of reprisals after disclosure. Most paedophiles and child rapists use threats of death or lies, such as a parent not believing them or stop loving them.

Threats are usually enough to keep the 'SECRET' safe. However, being able to tell a trusted individual what has happened in confidence, without being judged or given advice, can be the start of a powerful healing source.

Anger,

Anger is often underpinned by pain and frustration, at what happened, at those who may have disbelieved you. Sometimes anger can be called; the backbone of healing – a powerful and freeing force,

There are positive ways to channel this anger, physical activity, talking to someone you trust or a trained counsellor or trauma therapist. You can write a journal of your experience to alleviate the way you feel and transform those feelings into a healthier emotion.

Disbelief and shock – in the beginning it may have been hard to come to terms with what has happened and life may seem chaotic, you may go over and over scenes in your mind unable to shut it out.

These thoughts may take up one hundred per cent of your thinking time, leaving no space for anything else in your life. This can be distressing and disturbing to the balance of the mind. It is important to know that this will not last forever and it really is possible to put the pieces of your life back together and to move on.

Your mind is your healer, everything you need right now is within you - invest in searching.

Self-Blame

Rape and other sexually violating attacks whether perpetrated on a man, woman or child by a man, woman or a group of abusers is NEVER, EVER the survivors fault.

You may feel that you need to take the blame due to misplaced loyalties or thoughts such as:

'I must have done something to deserve it'

Well, you DID NOT deserve this; the only person/s to blame are the perpetrator/s.

Make Peace with your Inner Child (Girls)

Create a psychological first aid kit (in a pretty box/cloth bag that he/she could decorate which gives him/her something physical to hold).

This might be useful for him/her when she is struggling, if he/she is quite childlike and has difficulty talking about this, drawing his/her resources might be useful.

Listen to your inner voice – keep strong, become who you want to be, not who others want you to be......

Healing is not about people feeling sorry for you, which is why talking to friends or family does not always help. Healing is about regaining the power and control that has been taken away from you.

Healing and restoration of YOU...

There are excellent researched, proven techniques and interventions available for those who have suffered traumatic events and to enable lessening of the impact.

YOUR investment in YOU....

It really is important for you to know that it is completely possible to get through this and move on, you can assist your natural ability to heal both emotionally and physically.

The pain can be likened to s deepening barbed splinter and the more the innocent survivor tries to ignore it, the sharper the barbs become and the deeper the splinter goes, taking with it, searing emotional pain. With the right help, it IS possible to remove that splinter.

A New Growth

Visit a garden centre or plant nursery. Purchase your favourite tree, bush or whatever suits you and plant it somewhere significant to you – let it represent the **new you**, the **stronger you.**

Watch its' beauty emerge, just as the courage within you has emerged, restoring you.

You are stronger than you ever thought you could be. You will survive this and you will move on. Believe in yourself as you take every new step.

Healing and keeping emotionally safe....

It is important to love and honour yourself and to take care of your own needs at this time.

Sometimes you may need to find a way to ground yourself when you are feeling less than confident, panicky ...try the following grounding techniques.

1. Using the 7/11 breathing technique, breathe in a colour that makes you feel calm and in control.

2. Breathe out the colour that has the strongest association with the panic and fear.

3. Enjoy a further 15 – 30 minute breathing exercise.

4. Think about your Empowered Self grounding his/her self right now.

5. Listen to calming music/meditation.

6. Go for a brisk walk.

7. Power nap.

8. Plan your weekend.

9. Enjoy a nourishing meal or snack.

10. Telephone or text to family or friends.

11. Complete an exercise in this work book.

12. Do the crossword/word search

If it helps, make some notes under the options about the techniques that help you the most.....

EMPTY 'RAGE PAGE' EXERCISE......

Draw a picture of someone or something that has annoyed you today and rip
it up into tiny pieces – dispose of as you wish and move on.....

Now that you are coming to the end of the workbook

List ten ways that you have found to help yourself recover, that might be making an appointment to see a counsellor or support worker, it might be taking up a new activity that releases somatic (body memory) trauma. Or anything in fact that YOU believe has helped you along your pathway to recovery.

1.

2.

3.

4.

5.

6.

7.

8.

9.

10.

"And once the storm is over, you won't remember how you made it through, how you managed to survive.

You won't even be sure whether the storm is really over. But one thing is certain...

When you come out of the storm, you won't be the same person who walked in.

That's what this storm is all about".

Haruki Murakami – Kafka on the Shore
ISBN 1-84343-110-6

Crossword Answers (page 11).

Across

a. Bath

d. Ure

g. Ash

h. Opera

j. Skell

l. Can

m. Red

n. Cat

o. Eve

q. Pre

s. Koi

u. Error

w. Inset

x. Elm

y. ETA

z. Odes

Personal Reflective Journal Notes...

Other resources in this category, available to order from the Jigsaw Website www.traumaresources.co.uk or Amazon Online:

Heart Encounter – Audio CD

Like a tidal wave, the effects of childhood sexual abuse can saturate an adult throughout their life. This Guided Visualisation Audio CD has been produced to allow the choice of time and space in the safety in one's own environment where disturbance can be minimal and relaxation can be attained in order to feel the letting go of many painful memories.

The Splinter – Audio CD

This Guided Visualisation has been produced to assist those affected by rape and sexual violation to find some peace and release from what they have endured. This production is not intended to treat or cure any psychological response from the trauma of rape and sexual violence or assault. It is intended as a stepping-stone along the passage of healing and recovery.

Little Book of Strength – Pocket Book Self Help

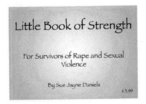

This Little Book of Strength is a useful visual tool for survivors of rape and sexual violence, prepared as a small wallet/purse size (7x10cm). A paperback booklet of healing and restoration for anyone who has been the target of a sexual perpetrator or has suffered a personal act of sexual violence whether as an adult or a child.

References

Griffin, J and Tyrrell, I (2001*). The Shackled Brain: how to release locked-in patterns of trauma.* HG Publishing, East Sussex.

Griffin, J Tyrrell, I (2006) *Human Givens Joe Griffin & Ivan Tyrell* (HG Publishing)

Van der Kolk BA, *The compulsion to repeat the trauma: re-enactment, revictimisation, and masochism.* Psychiatr Clin North Am 1989; 12(2):389-411.

Angelou, Maya (1978) Excerpt from *And Still I Rise.* Virago Press Ltd (London); 1st.Ed.1978, Reprinted1999 (8th) edition (8 May 1986)

Daniels, Sue J, (2011) *Quote - We each make our own prison.*

Angelou, Maya (2008) *Letter to My Daughter:* Publisher: Virago; Reprint edition (4 Oct. 2012)

Van Gogh, Vincent (1883) *Vincent van Gogh. Letter to Theo Van Gogh. 28 October 1883 in Drenthe.* Translated by Mrs. Johanna van Gogh-Bonger, edited by Robert Harrison, number 336

Churchill, Winston (2003) The Prodigal Project: Book 1: Genesis. Publisher: Plume (1 Jan. 2002)

Murakami, Haruki. Kafka on the Shore: *Kafka Tamura runs away from home at fifteen, under the shadow of his father's dark prophecy.* Publisher: Vintage. New Ed edition (6 Oct. 2005)

Made in the USA
Columbia, SC
18 December 2020